Being a Good Citizen

by John Serrano

What Does a Good Citizen Do?

A good citizen helps other people. A good citizen cares about other people, too.

Good citizens are kind and tell the truth. They work hard and respect others.

How Can You Be a Good Citizen at Home?

You can be a good citizen by helping at home. You can wash the dishes and sweep the floor.

Look at this boy. He is a good citizen. He helps take care of his dog.

▲ This boy is helping at home.

You can be kind to your brothers and sisters.

You can also use kind words when you speak. “Please” and “thank you” are kind words.

▲ These sisters get along well.

How Can You Be a Good Citizen at School?

You can be a good citizen by following the rules. You can wait your turn to speak.

You can listen to what other people say. A good citizen listens to the teacher, too.

▲ Students who listen are good citizens.

You can follow rules in the halls, too. You can speak softly in the halls.

You can walk instead of run. A good citizen works hard to keep the school safe and clean.

▲ Good citizens are proud of their school.

How Can You Be a Good Citizen in Your Town?

You can be a good citizen by showing that you care about your town.

You can help keep the town clean. A good citizen makes less trash.

▲ These good citizens pick up trash.

You can help people in your town. Some people do not have enough food and clothing.

A good citizen collects food and clothing for people who don't have enough.

▲ These good citizens give food to people who don't have enough.

You can be a good citizen in many places. You can be a good citizen everywhere you go!